IN THE HERE AND NOW

PREVIOUS BOOKS BY JANET MONTEFIORE

Poetry
Shaping Spirits, Shoestring Press 2016
Disposing of the Clothes, Shoestring Press 2019

IN THE HERE AND NOW

Selected Poems 1975–2023

JANET MONTEFIORE

All rights reserved. No part of this work covered by the copyright herein may be reproduced or used in any means – graphic, electronic, or mechanical, including copying, recording, taping, or information storage and retrieval systems – without written permission of the publisher.

Printed by imprintdigital
Upton Pyne, Exeter
imprintdigital.com

Typesetting and cover design by The Book Typesetters
hello@thebooktypesetters.com
07422 598 168
thebooktypesetters.com

Published by Shoestring Press
19 Devonshire Avenue, Beeston, Nottingham, NG9 1BS
(0115) 925 1827
shoestringpress.co.uk

First published 2024
© Copyright: Janet Montefiore
© Cover photograph: Winding Pond in Clowes Wood, Blean, East Kent by Janet Montefiore

The moral right of the author has been asserted.

ISBN 978-1-915553-54-6

ACKNOWLEDGEMENTS

'What I told the dead man' first appeared in *Stand* (titled 'Dreams after childbirth'). Earlier versions of 'Can I get there by candlelight?', 'Two poems after Sappho', 'Quiet consummation' and 'Last words' were first published in *Logos: The UKC Literary Magazine*. 'Another time', 'Thresholds' and 'Cuckoo-flowers' appeared in *PN Review*, 'Going' in *Orbis*, 'Disposing of the Clothes' in *English*, and 'Night visitor' in the *TLS*. 'Falling leaves' first appeared *in Time Present and Time Past: Poets at the University of Kent, 1965-1985* ed. Robyn Bolam (Yorick Books 1985). 'A state occasion' first appeared in *Spare Rib*, and 'Feathered the bed of nightmare' in *Agenda*. 'Mass-rock in Co. Waterford' first appeared in *Jellyfish Cupful: Writings in Honour of John Fuller*, eds. Barney Cokeliss and James Fenton (Ulysses, 1997), and an earlier version of 'Women writers of the 1930s' in *Women's Writing of the 1930s*, ed. Mary Joannou (Edinburgh University Press, 1999). 'If' was first published in *Poems for the Binsted Prize: An Anthology* ed. Camilla Lambert (South Downs Poetry Festival and Binsted Arts, 2021).

For Patrick Cockburn
with love

CONTENTS

What I told the dead man	1
Can I get there by candlelight?	2
Pastry people	3
Another time	4
Going	6
Thresholds	7
Cuckoo-flowers	9
Two poems after Sappho	10
If	11
Shell dreams	12
Quiet consummation	13
Night visitor	14
Last words	15
Disposing of the clothes	16
Falling leaves	17
Mass-rock in Co. Waterford	18
What mothers do: Canterbury and Baghdad 1991	19
A state occasion	21
Fighting words	22
Illustration	23
Objections from a subject	24
Message received	26
Love poem	27
Feathered the bed of nightmare	28
Winter flowering	30
The Lecturer's Dream	32
Reader's Guide	42
Illuminations 1776–1991	44
Occasional Poems	46
John Betjeman biking the Greenway, between showers	51
Notes	53

WHAT I TOLD THE DEAD MAN

Sleepless, thirsty, in pain from my stitched leaking body
in a half-waking doze, I seemed to be handling shells,
rainbow-coloured, blue, purple, white: curved and whorled
    and scalloped,
intricate, bewildering and tiny, to be sorted into heaps
for my mother-in-law's workbox. There were brilliant blue cowries
small white curving jaw-bones like flat delicate horns,
tiny mauve needles, coarse black thorns and scratchy pink
    fragile fruits
(sea-urchins, these) and deep rose spirals.
I put them in order carefully, as when Psyche sorted her grains,
and sleep was poured on my eyelids, a dark deep stream
down which I floated to meet a dead man with hooded eyes
    and bloodless lips
but a flicker of life still in him. I told him my tale,
the induction, the waters breaking, the long (or it seemed long)
    first stage of labour
and the too-early-born leg stirring strangely, and the controlled
    rush to the operating theatre,
and the numbness below my breasts where the surgeon was
    rummaging for the baby,
and his triumphant entrance. So I told the dead man
how his grandson was born, pouring out language not blood,
and I saw it meant nothing though he listened patiently, with a
    decent pretence
of interest. Dear ghost, his mind was elsewhere,
on his own dissolution, as the deep river ran into darkness.

CAN I GET THERE BY CANDLELIGHT?

Bright windows at dusk, that means a party,
convivial spirits and my lost mother

shelling peas in the kitchen almost like herself,
her fingers recovering skill and intention

though she cannot speak. Sweet fields lie beyond
dressed in living green, and a sea aflame

with sunset, where further off Elizabeth Bishop
is waiting for the boat to bring her to the party,

rowed by a small boy across the swelling flood.
The telephone rings. It's Elizabeth, hoping

the boat comes soon, asking politely
may she be our guest until the darkness lightens?

PASTRY PEOPLE

She lifts her truncheon, brown and slightly sticky,
dusts it with flour, pressing the pastry down,
rolling it flat, cutting it, fitting it
to match the pie-dish. She balls the oddments, flattens,
cuts them to leaf-shapes, knifing the veins neatly.

We finger the left-over scraps,
roll them grey and sticky into snakes and balls,
snakes halved for the limbs, a squashed ball for the body,
a smaller for the face. Currant eyes and buttons.

We cook them hard and hot, the buttons fallen off
the tummies, the sweetness burnt out of the eyes
and eat them without relish, while her creation
bakes to its elegant brown, its rich mess of gravy.

ANOTHER TIME
for E.M.M.

My mother's face is a tombstone – blank, but for a few
semi-legible lines.
                        In loving memory?
So I like to believe. But how can I guess what
if anything, she recalls?
                        Sun and shade play
over her weathered surface – puzzlement, distress,
a long empty stare, a momentary half-smile,
equal, unreadable.
                        Words are gone,
vanished in the dark of her skull, as if they never were.
There remain only fragments
                        Can you tell me? followed
by a jumble of syllables. We can tell her nothing.
Her eyes, sunk in their pits, see us without knowledge
and without love.
                        In another time
she loved language, and the world: Orion ravishing the skies,
finches and brindled cows, burning tiger, water-snakes
coiling their fiery tracks, and the psalms she made us read
about the just man who keeps his word *even though it were
to his own hindrance*, and the Lord whose *ministers
are a flaming fire*.
                        In another time
she showed me a crocus, outshone by the purple clusters
around it – but this one, creamy-pale
striped black, smelt of honey, she said.
                        It was true,
the crocus full of strong scent. In another time
lost now beneath the white lines of her hair

combed by kindly nurses, under the dark caves
where her eyes are sunk, behind her broken teeth and warm lips
that still form bits of words. Which may not be empty,
whose truth is locked in another time.

GOING

"Now that your mother only needs nightdresses,"
my father calls me to ask, "which of her clothes would you like?"
Why am I so horrified? I delight in
my mother-in-law's Chinese coat, I wear her anorak,
Claud's blackthorn stick still has the feel of his hand,
dead more than fifteen years. But Mum's tweed coat,
her gloves and shawls – even the thought of them
gives me gooseflesh. Do I think they're bad luck,
could eat away my memory, as hers has been eaten,
leaving only the grinding of teeth?

                                      Not quite.
They are her and not-her, as she is not herself.

                     O, let me go, let me go
she would chant under her breath, over and over,
when her speech was first going. Her prayer was answered
(she is gone) but withheld (she is still here).

But I have her letters. Her spiky handwriting
answered mine once: *nous n'irons plus au bois,
les lauriers sont coupés.*

                  I don't need her coat and gloves
to go to that wood where the words lie ruined
where a desolate pond reflects nothing but blankness
and a sweating beast trembles *O, let me go.*

THRESHOLDS

Fragments of the literal:
                    the beach where we walked,
the rocks where we sat, smooth to see and rough to touch:
   great whales which did not move in the waters,
the cactus pleased with the morning light standing tall among
   weeds,
vulture pecking a dead gull   broken bamboo I leant on,
dull sky over trodden sand   foam moving in sunlight

                            These are only fragments.
It was not like water darkening the red granite
                         varium et mutabile semper
not like brilliant Audenesque surfers swooping and tumbling
   past the rocks
not like the endless movement of the sea
                    trembling   invading   retreating.
We were not swimmers. Or not that kind.

                                  Rio, then?
where the sea is polluted   shit soup, they call it
and the sand filthy but silver at night
patterned with a slowly moving crowd of figures
beggars hustlers tourists   the cripples invisible
dim line of surf marking unseen ocean
inaudible behind the homeless roar of traffic

darkness and distance   a crowd but no actors
no, it was not remotely like the city by the sea

But some fragments I have still   shells we found in the sand
iridescent mussels   intricately patterned limpet a tiny knobbly
   oyster
others shaped like the wings of a butterfly   striped and

    banded purple and green
signifiers of the dead woman who taught me to name them
                                and of dreams after childbirth
empty homes   salt and bitter jewels

They are on my table now gleaming in lamplight
                                       keeping a faint taste of salt
That time   I arranged them on the palm of my hand
as we spoke of pain and loss, children and childlessness
                             I watched the movement of my
                                                                skin
unbalancing the neat piles
                 Yes, bitter jewels

Marginal spaces   sea's movement
   across red granite   two women talking
broken shells

CUCKOO-FLOWERS

When I spoke to her shadow it sometimes answered.
More often she was silent. Once I thought I held her
but my body wasn't fooled. Or not for long.
Tossing and turning with shut eyes, it knew the sign was empty.

I dreamed a couplet for her, but its words
seemed like a quotation
>
> *and the cuckoo-flower*
> *choked in snow*

This is how I read it: the flower is pleasure
which the snow stifles. Clear enough: desire
frozen into silence

Then an image without words, a single
wallflower bloom   deep yellow streaked with crimson
a little past its best   but bright   soft   scented
petals spread backwards   an unspeakable pleasure

TWO POEMS AFTER SAPPHO

(i) Evening star

Brilliant planet in March dusk, glimpsed through ugly light
of orange street-lamps blurring shadows, you bring home a
    queue of cars
in a dazzling fuming snake-trail, bring a mother from an
    emptied building
filling with darkness and silence, home to the yellow glimmer
edging curtained windows, to light left on for wakeful children.

(ii) Moonset

The woman late at night, when half-lit ivory doors swing wide
finds herself quick as thought close to a slender body
that slides into to her arms, fluidly as a fish
leaping and re-entering darkness. So for a passing second
she is present, poised to embrace, like a naked boy at bath-time
balancing on the rim, arms and legs spread wide
like Leonardo's man, water-dropped hands and feet
exactly meeting the corners of the towel held out for him.
But the waters run away, and what was a clear dark pool
is only a white bath-tub hollow as an empty shell,
the flow and sparkle gone. And the cheated arms stretch
to the passing empty hours and a vanishing image.

IF

If I could give you these –

gorse yellow as buttercups on the Méséglise way,
tiger-striped snails probing grass-stems with elegant sexy horns,
samphire bushes hanging from the rocks,
nasturtiums close by, forget-me-not's outline (I don't forget
                        you) shadowed on an orange trumpet,
rippling blue streaked with paler paths, darkened with purple
                        cloud-shadows, edged with creamy white
where invisible rocks are engulfed, caressed and dragged,
                        flooded and worn away,
ship crossing an inch between two pansies,
insects simmering in the fuchsia hedge, ants traversing my page
attacking my bare foot, stinging me into the here and now –

If they were mine to give

SHELL DREAMS

In a January wood I picked up a snail-shell
worn pale and mould-speckled among dead leaves,
which multiplied that night into half-open mussels
under my fingers. These, I was told
by a voice that seemed to know, were the eggs of hedgehogs
laid in earth by males of the species
whose babies, all male, would hatch out in spring,
(a parthenogenesis known only in hedgehogs).

A brown damp embryo was already stirring
in his open shell, and would die of the cold
unless I tucked him in my bra (which being a feminist
I don't usually wear), and within that warmth
might lack proper food, for I could only foster
not feed him. Yet he would achieve definition
growing quick and lively on his diet of dreams.

QUIET CONSUMMATION
i.m. Sarah Cockburn 1939–2000

It wasn't time for you to come to dust
but time took you early, shrivelling in silence
dusty and deathly as the smoke from your pipe
up the Mortlake chimney, while Shakespeare's dirge was spoken,
true for everybody, harshly true of you.

'Care no more to clothe and eat,'
whose dresses were holed with tobacco burns
and by the end, could barely swallow.

Oh, I know you live on in your books –
the tax inspector knifed in a Venice bedroom,
the ugly girl thrown off a financier's balcony,
the witch and her golden boy lured to death by water,

but I miss your laughter, your tobacco-stained fingers,
the *Chambers Dictionary* you lost under your bed
while doing *The Times* crossword you never missed,
not even the day you died, the wineglass you filled me,
the Shakespeare plays we'll never talk about again.

NIGHT VISITOR

So many people pass through the ward, no one
will notice me, I think, opening a door
on darkness, silence and a shaft of light
entering a window. The patients are asleep,
humped dark shapes, all but one naked back
rising out of the bedclothes, white and smooth
in the moonlight as a Rodin marble, intent
on sleep, not love – man, woman? I can't tell,
the head's cradled in shadows, unknowable
as the other bodies. Which are not at peace,
have suffered, will again, and if I'm careless now
will wake to pain, but for this one bare hour
keep their shared solitude, as in a library
full of absorbed readers. To that place,
though I'm dreaming too, I have no entrance ticket.

LAST WORDS

Remembrance Sunday when my mother went
(it was my birthday, I was fifty-one)
ended, I thought, a life already gone.
Feeling and intelligence were dead.
Visited in the geriatric ward,
she'd grind her teeth for hours as she gazed
through us as blankly as a window-pane,
a dark cottage with nobody inside.

But she would prove me wrong the day my father
sitting with her a week before her death,
saw the door open. He heard her speak his name,
'You're Hugh and I love you,' his dear Eliza
back just long enough to say to him
the only words that mattered as she left.

DISPOSING OF THE CLOTHES

Lying inside his coffin, he was robed –
dog-collar, purple cassock, but no ring
silver-gilt with its embossed *Chi-Rho*,
my sister's keeping that, his bishop's bling.
His mitres, stoles and cope we gave away,
the cloth of gold, lawn sleeves and orange velvet
embroidery went to the U.S.P.G.,
some other bishop will be glad to wear it,

but not his baggy blue sweater and trousers,
not even Oxfam would have wanted those.
And when his house was stripped, I asked the movers
who'd cleared the rooms of sofas, books and sermons
to leave Pa's anorak hanging by the stairs
ready for one more walk on Wandsworth Common.

FALLING LEAVES
after Horace

Autumn, when the gardener sweeps and tidies.
The leaves gleaming on October grass,
not more blond than himself
at twenty, though a balding head
can hardly compare with the stripped
elegance of winter branches.

Smoke streaks off the heaped leaves
in yellowish-grey tendrils
curled then dissolved by the wind.
For whom does he comb this hair?
The pretty boy dripping with scent
will lounge among the roses
next summer, with a new friend.

October gales sweep the trees
bringing another flaky damp shower.
Sit in a warm room with a drink
and watch the gardener struggle.

MASS-ROCK IN CO. WATERFORD

Invisible, not hidden – you reach it by a track
marked on the government map, where you leave the cliff path
to climb down steep ledges to a shallow
grassy dell narrowing to an overhang
above a gulf of rock, squawks of gulls
and far below, the sea.
                          Here, where the stone
turns reddish, are the legends – names carved wherever
you set your foot: *O'Connell, Fitzgerald, Henesy,
Sarah Coghlan Bristol*, elegantly lettered, dated
Jan.y 1st 1848, inside her chiselled rectangle
(a local beauty who paid a stone-cutter
for those shapely letters?), a crudely done shamrock
three feet across, flaking and weed-cracked, sloping
down to the falling waves.
                             Though I've been told these names
go back three centuries, speaking of Ninety-Eight,
of the Penal Times and masses said in secret,
most are far later.
                    And still signify exile.
Sarah Coghlan bound for her Bristol groom, Connolly
in 1852 after the Famine, O'Brien in 1935, others more recent
incised themselves where rain, salt wind, gulls roosting,
flaking rocks, spreading crust of lichen, seeds rooting in cracks,
clumps of grass and white campion, scrape of visiting feet,
everything that says *Eire*, slowly erode the names.

WHAT MOTHERS DO: CANTERBURY AND BAGHDAD 1991

As the TV winks and chatters, our son who should be asleep
is playing with Lego, not knowing yet that his journalist father
has gone back to the war zone, which is partly why I'm watching.
I have to tell him tomorrow, though I dread his fearful question
What if they bomb Daddy's hotel in Baghdad?
and the nightmares that have left him sitting upright and
    wide-eyed
apparently seeing nothing, panicked rigid and sweaty,
crying out broken words. But now he is playing, oblivious
it seems, to the news story (later called 'unpatriotic')
showing Iraqi victims. First an old woman shouting
in furious Arabic, subtitled English: *Will destroying our houses
get the army out of Kuwait?*
                              And now a boy lying still
on the ground, about ten years old, his mother sitting beside him,
ignoring the men who have come, risking disapproval or worse
to report the wreck of her life. Her face stares out of the screen
in our bright untidy room, the face of someone trapped
in a bad dream, her son broken past help or comfort,
and still she stays by his side, doing what mothers do.
Maybe the father's a soldier in that Iraqi army
we're about to drive from Kuwait like dead leaves before our wind,
having blown apart these lesser lives.
                                      The camera moves back
to show some Western newsmen. There (and this is not a dream)
stands my husband, looking down at the boy and silent mother
his face twisted in pity – and suddenly our son
glances up, perhaps alerted by my own dismay
at his father watching this Iraqi *pietà* strangely carried
on sightless couriers of the airwaves into our English house.
But he returns to his Lego, apparently seeing nothing,
and I say nothing to him, tears will not drown that wind.

I put the boy to bed, tuck him in safe and warm,
wait for his breathing to quieten, doing what mothers do.

A STATE OCCASION

The knives are waiting and the candles lit.
Under the heat, the blister slowly swells
While joints crack open, turning on the spit.

Gas-ovens have replaced the charcoal pit;
Inventiveness is where our race excels.
The knives are waiting and the candles lit.

Necessity demands that bones should split.
Reasons of state exhale their kitchen smells
While joints crack open, turning on the spit.

The red-faced book surveys his juicy bit
Where blood-drops run inside the secret cells.
The knives are waiting and the candles lit.

Our cheerful gentry exercise their wit:
Who can eat eggs and not have broken shells?
While joints crack open, turning on the spit.

A public meal few private mouths admit.
What eating means, what's eaten rarely tells.
The knives are waiting and the candles lit
While joints crack open, turning on the spit.

FIGHTING WORDS

If I should speak, what word would I unlock?
The old offender pleading in the dock
Hinting obscurities that interweave
An alibi which no one can believe.
Enter the judge to read the charges filed.
Correction please, enter a bloody child.
Her smile displays a white and gleaming hedge
Where meaning hides the darkness of its edge,
Actions divide and metaphors condense.
Behind the lips, behind the ivory fence,
I hear my speech uncensored and entire.

ILLUSTRATION

A trail of foliage makes a suitable border
with crimson and orange birds perching
on its delicate lines. Inside, top left,
a miniature icon,

a room with a figure seated at a table
enclosed on three sides by retreating bookshelves.
At the window we look through, ivy is curling,
a spider is weaving.

There are pen and paper, so we know this is a writer.
Lying on the table is a book, entitled
(but you need a magnifying glass to read it)
A Lover's Discourse.

OBJECTIONS FROM A SUBJECT

This place is covered with likenesses
of me – all recognisable, but none of them
seems quite accurate. Not that they're untrue:
I can see myself in each and perhaps,
collectively, they add up to a truth
but not, if so, one that interests me,

which is embarrassing, since your interest in me
clearly, is responsible for these images
like windows constructed to let in daylight
but only reflecting – one can't see through them.
Even my narcissism has its limits, despite
appearances. And the mirrors are distorted

though how could it be otherwise? Deception
is inevitable. It's the insistence on myself
that I find impossible to take, although
the loving skill that created these images
is impressive, and I could be grateful for them,
they have their own kind of reality

and very honestly don't pretend to be true.
I enjoy the picture of myself as deceiver,
the observant eyes with no trust in them,
the hand drawing dishevelled silk across my
delicate white bosom, and this portrait –
more like a cartoon really – myself as mother, but

hardly a madonna: remorseless, cruel even
to the whining child whose features accurately
represent your own. A lacerating likeness
literally, for in this caricature
your supplicating hands are clutching me
flinching as my fingernails lightly scratch them.

I am tired of these likenesses, all of them,
even the blossoming girl, who is flattering but
like the rest, wearies me with myself.
If you make, as you do, no claims to truthfulness
I am not contained in your acknowledged error.
Could you live yourself in such a hall of mirrors?

MESSAGE RECEIVED

Distanced by several countries and six weeks,
I send my love tonight in your direction.
It's all too likely though to meet obstruction
Across so many forests, cities, peaks.
Good citizens may feel what's meant for you
And wonder why this beam of energy
Deriving from an unknown personality
Should suddenly be taking an undue
Interest in them, however warm and friendly.
Recipients report: 'We feel oppressed.
Its concentration makes us all embarrassed,
We don't like being looked at so intently.
   What made it long for us we cannot say.
   We wish politely it would go away.'

LOVE POEM

Cold explorer, disappear
    Into the mountains of your mind:
    Rocky paths where reasons wind,
Icy pools where thought is clear.

Move the inch that brings you near –
    Down in the hidden valley deep
    Lie warm, lie gentle, lie asleep,
Known and knowing, strange and dear.

FEATHERED THE BED OF NIGHTMARE

Feathered the down that fills the quilt
that covers the bed of nightmare

Feathered the bird whose death is guilt
that shed the down that fills the quilt
that covers the bed of nightmare

Feathered the sky with icy down
as light as mist as cold as stone
that fills the air when the bird has gone
the fluttering bird whose death is guilt
whose feathers are plucked to stuff the quilt
that covers the bed of nightmare

Feathered the pane of icy glass
covered with fronds of branching frost
that blanches breath and brings down cloud
to flake and drift in a pale cold shroud
that climbs the wall to the window-sill
filling the room with deathly chill
where the sleeper shudders beneath a quilt
stuffed with the barbs of mortal guilt
that lies on the heart of nightmare

Feathered the breast all white and warm
of the bird that flew in the howling storm
that covered the world in a cold white shroud
for the innocent bird whose life was spilled
feathered the arrow that maimed and killed

piercing the flesh as the marksman willed
and the wounded breastbone bled and thrilled
of the warm white bird whose death is guilt
that shed the down as soft as silk
that smothers the bed of nightmare

Feathered and sharp the grey goose-quill
dripping black ink like a greedy bill
that feathered the arrow that pierced and killed
the bird whose breast is bloody and chilled
and feathered the sky with drifting down
as white as mist and as cold as stone
and feathered the pane of icy glass
with abstract patterns of branching frost
that bleaches breath and thickens cloud
to crystallise in a colourless shroud
that lies on the heart all cold with guilt
that feathered the down that fills the quilt
that covers the bed of nightmare

WINTER FLOWERING
i.m. D.J.E.

When hailstones scatter coldest corn
    Across the unploughed brine,
And freezing gales hiss through the wreck
    Of elm and ruined pine,
When hoar-frost spreads its icy net
    On leafless stalk and spine,

The brightness of your golden flowers
    Answers the winter sun
Whose noonday warmth brings out your scent
    As rich and sweet as June
When grace and toughness counterpoint
    Prickliness with perfume.

And yet these pleasures give themselves
    Only to scent and eye.
Exploring hands encounter spikes,
    Noli me tangere.
Bad luck will come to anyone
    Reckless enough to try.

The melting frost that furred your thorns
    Flashes in green and rose,
Brilliant and trembling as a star
    Until the sunlight goes
Leaving a frigid glassy bead
    Which night will crystallise

For now the evening chill comes on
    Warning me I should go
Back to the cosy lighted house
    Which is forbidden you,
Inhabitant of darkness
Darker than I can know.

THE LECTURER'S DREAM

"Thus author, metaphorically, is father,
    The Book, his heir. As every reader knows…."
I simply couldn't read it any farther,
    My horn-rimmed spectacles slid down my nose.
A slumber did my spirit seal – or rather,
    A numbing torpor did my eyelids close.
Upon the text my weary forehead slumped,
And sleepy images within it bumped.

Swirled by a powerful current which connoted
    Ancestral tides of long-forgotten seas,
Through thickly flowing dark canals I floated
    With boneless monsters, bringers of disease
And things that ate them, fat and white and bloated.
    I left them there, determined I would seize
The first hold I could find, and climbed a stair,
Steep as a ladder, white and knobbly, where

I glimpsed a flickering form and called out "Hey,
    Stetson! What are you doing here in this illogical
Strange world?" It answered coldly, "Patience, pray.
    That's the wrong poem. I'm a Mythological
Entity, and your guide." – "Then will you say
    What you are called?" –"I am a Mythological
Entity, as I told you," mopping and mowing,
"We all have names like that, where you are going."

This Being was unusually designed:
        It wore a wreath of laurel on Its head;
Its right hand clasped a golden bough, with nine
        Dependent silver apples, and there led
A cord from this whose coiling knots entwined
        A white hound with (you've guessed it) ears of red.
Its robe was purple, and to my eyes odd,
A cross between a Vegetation-God

And a Death-Spirit. "Stop that silly staring,"
   It said, moving up quickly, so I followed
On the white ladder, once I'd got my bearing,
   Till the white hound broke loose – we yelled and holloa'd
(After some leucocyte the brute went haring)
   Till it returned. We climbed, until a hollowed
Chamber received us. "Here we are," It said,
"We've reached our goal – the inside of your head."

A strange, uncanny sense of *déjà-vu*
   Came over me as both of us stood gazing.
Surely I know that catalogue, that blue
   Round ceiling, and that drowsy person lazing
Over his volumes? Yes, of course I do –
   Or if I don't, this place has an amazing
Resemblance to –"Oh, no!" I clutched my guide,
"Is *that* what my poor skull is like inside,

The B.M. Reading Room?" It was an ugly
   Surprise. "Don't get upset," It said, adjusting
The laurel wreath, as I thought somewhat smugly,
   "Doesn't that demonstrate your mind's not rusting?"
"Oh, yeah?" – "Don't worry, thoughts are sleeping snugly
   In corners of your cortex we're not thrusting
Into tonight. But now look – I assure you
The people in the Reading Room won't bore you."

They didn't. For assembled here were writers
    Who normally stayed quietly on the shelves:
Meredith, Peacock (obviously as tight as
    A tick) and the great novelists themselves
Whose works from Sterne to Isherwood delight us,
    And Tolkien sitting with a group of elves,
And who's that codger like an angry owl?
Evelyn Waugh's face, twisting in a scowl

At Huxley, whom he's far from pleased to find
    In here; Joyce and Lawrence the Primal Force,
And Proust who by the look of him has dined
    With someone whom he finds a trifle coarse,
And here's George Eliot radiating Mind,
    And Balzac, who's lost thousands on the Bourse ...
"You're right, these certainly are most exciting
To watch – but Entity, why aren't they writing?"

"Even upon Parnassus," It replied,
    "There has to be a time for relaxation,
So sometimes from their work these turn aside
    To find some less demanding occupation –
Knitting or Scrabble. All of them have tried
    Some remedy for constant cerebration
(Except Flaubert, he's tougher than a camel is).
They're now at Literary Happy Families."

One riffles through her cards, and "Mr Waugh,
    Can you please give me Master Neatly Ironic?
And Richly Human?" – "No, but I'll thank you for,
    Miss Murdoch, two Suggestives and one Comic."
Intangibly, Profoundly and one more,
    Sir Richly Comic pass, and Sir Sardonic
Humour (from Peacock). But he comes a cropper
Demanding Comic Anecdote from Sapper.

(The strain of keeping up *ottava rima*
   Has tempted me to slack half-rhyming ways:
Apologies from your distracted dreamer.)
   Jane Austen's turn, and as you'd guess, she plays
A wily game, getting a Moral Theme, a
   Symbolic Paradox (a card that pays
Double) and Biting Irony from Dickens,
At which a vein upon his temple thickens.

Several more rounds of shuffling, dealing, joking
   Continue, till abruptly William Thackeray
Accuses Dostoyevsky of revoking.
   "Either that idiot's drunk and lost his knack, or he's
Cheating outright and monstrously provoking.
   He damned well ought to give me my turn back, or he
Should leave. – You *have* got Mr Starkly Abrasive."
"*I* didn't know," says Fyodor, evasive.

"It says so somewhere in a master's thesis."
   He takes one down, and flicking through – "It's in
Here somewhere … Film montage compared with *tmesis*?
   No, that's not it." –"Why don't you stick a pin
At random?" a jeer that demonstrates Makepeace is
   Not his right middle name. The ensuing din
And fisticuffs aroused the spectral hound
To snap his leash and with a joyous bound

Jump out and bite Turgenev in the ankle.
   We hauled him back and beat a quick retreat:
The Russians seemed inclined to let it rankle.
   "Can't you control your dog?" "Oh no, he's sweet!
And I've no doubt his harmless little prank'll
   Be forgotten soon. – "You are an effete
Entity," I very nearly said
But prudence won; I shut my mouth instead.

It was my guide; I didn't want to fight.
   "Well then," said I, "what next? We can't go back."
"Certainly not, we're not half through the night.
   And you, my friend, have yet another pack
Of cards to play before the morning light.
   Follow my footsteps close and mark my track.
Keep your perceptions bright and clean and sharp; it
'S not all who see the figure in the carpet."

"But what have we to do with Henry James?"
   "Nothing, we left the novelists behind.
We're bound for further literary games
   Which busy neurones shuffle in your mind.
You saw the cards?'- "All those amazing names,
   Could I forget them?" "Good. So now you'll find
The terminologies come off the cards,
Appear as people and no longer words."

"Incarnate, is it?" –"Yes." – "I still don't get it."
   "Watch." As It spoke, there swam into my sight
Something I knew, though not sure where I'd met it:
   A wispy girl in draperies, with light
Untidy hair escaping from its net – it
   Was straggling somewhat. Though her eyes were bright,
Their gaze was strangely distant. I'd have guessed if
It asked, this was Intangibly Suggestive.

Sir Richly Human next, his coat plumped roundly.
   Distributing choc-ices and baked beans
To children, he deserves the title soundly.
   And that young man in faded velvet jeans
And deep abstraction, he must be Profoundly
   Suggestive. (Do not think this sentence leans
Askew; I merely used a little *zeugma*:
To rhetoricians this is no enigma.)

I see Profoundly's followed by a frolic –
　　If I may term it so – of mystic beasts:
A Moral Theme, not one to sing or rollick,
　　A long thin worm in spectacles, whose feasts
Are purely cerebral. The Parabolic
　　Enigma's with it: who knows what strange yeasts
Ferment in that impenetrable cloud?
It has no face and cannot speak aloud –

"What other way would you expect it to,
　　You pleonast! And do you know it can't?"
My guide said crossly. "Calm yourself, now do.
　　What's *that* one?" – "Well, no mineral nor plant
But such a strange beast as I never knew,
　　Unreal as the nuts in *Charlie's Aunt*.
Composed of hard, metallic, equilateral
Multi-dimensioned triangles symmetrical,

Conversing with its master in high squeaks –
　　A sort of Morse, but clearly it is mystical,
Singing through all its sixty angled beaks
　　A harmony both complex and sophistical.
Profoundly has the oddest set of freaks."
　　"You critics are excited and simplistic, all,"
Growled Entity, "it surely should be clear
That a Symbolic Paradox is here."

"You might be more polite." But now they came
　　Flocking: Sir Savage Irony, dark-haired
And grim; then Starkly Abrasive, his lean frame
　　Encased in sandpaper – this one was paired
With Neatly Ironic, playing some sharp game
　　Of ambiguities they cut and pared.
And here – her plump breasts strained her duffle-toggles
Came Ms Imagination Frankly Boggles

(Known to her friends as Madge) in a Mercedes
  Driven by Racy Gusto – rather flash.
He'd surely got the brightest of the ladies
  And looked the kind of chap to cut a dash.
"I didn't," said my guide, "come here from Hades
  To show you all these people, but the clash
Of types. For all these people interact,
Their differences are an important fact."

"I see you speak the language. But go on."
  "There are two sides, the Highbrow and the Low:
The Gustos and the Humorous upon
  One side, and the Suggestives" – "Yes, I know:
This is a ploy familiar to the don.
  And all the Ironies, where do they go?"
"Mostly to High." – "Sir Richly and Ms Boggles?"
"He's in the middle; as for her, she joggles.

"Sometimes she leans to Gusto, and sometimes
  Cleaves to Profoundly, for she's often fascinated
By his strange depths and the great heights he climbs,
  And by the dark, romantically lacerated
Features of Irony – and then at times
  The marinaded, wine-and-brandy-macerated
Topside of Richly Human." – "And Intangibly?"
"Attractions come to her more vague and frangibly:

She mostly drifts around with the Enigma."
  (He's landed me a very nasty rhyme:
I cannot think of anything but Stigma ,
  Or a small boy being told that now it's time
For bed, protesting "O, you are a pig, Ma!"
  Then let this stanza be a paradigm
Of clumsy metrical and rhymed incompetence
And with this final line then we can dump it hence.)

It's certainly an interesting crowd
    Of types and figures to be introduced to,
Like that young girl and gentleman in loud
    Checked tweeds: Intangibly has been induced to
Chat with Sir Richly Human. She is bowed
    And whispering – poor girl, she isn't used to
This, I can see. What's up, what are they doing?
"The plot is thickening, the broth is brewing.

Look over there – you see?" Behind their backs
    Are Racy Gusto and the Comic twins,
Grimly and Darkly, fingering their packs
    Of razors. *They* don't even have hat-pins.
They wait and wonder how long the attack's
    In coming. Nervously, Sir R. begins
A tentative approach – negotiations?
No – shrugs and smiles and mocking consolations.

Things don't look good – can nothing save our pair?
    Yes, look! A dim grey cloud has just descended:
The Parabolic Enigma fills the air
    With damp confusion, and as it intended
The two escape. Intangibly's long hair
    Is ruffled, and her skirt-hem must be mended,
That's all. Sir Richly eyes her sadly, turns,
Puffs his cigar; the end more greyly burns.

Now other groupings pass before my eyes:
    Ms Frankly-Boggles courted by Abrasive
While Savage Irony, in thin disguise
    As Humour, watched to see if they'd embrace, if
She'd …But Ms Boggles saw through his disguise
    And at her most expansive and persuasive
Charmed the two jealous lovers into singing
Duets harmonious, lyrical and ringing.

Each of these groups creates a situation:
    Profoundly with the Comic boys? A plot
Must be afoot. An odd association
    Like Moral Theme with Racy Gusto – what
Can that mean? "So your cerebral creation,"
    My guide resumed, "invents things that are not.
Each of these groups you've seen: now re-describe it.
Attach it back to literature. Ascribe it."

"But how?" – "Each group invokes a classic book
    And represents its individual qualities,
So which is which?" – "But Entity, now look,
    I can't – do you not see what total folly 'tis
To try and judge the cakes when I'm the cook,
    To be the audience of my own jollities?
And you can't tell if I am wrong or right
Since I invented you as well tonight."

"How do you know? We Entities go where
    We like. But no, you can't play games in dreams.
Try it when you're awake. You nearly are.
    Look where the light in yonder windows gleams.
The iris glass will open on the air
    Into the light, away from the dark streams."
Entity and Its hound now barely stained
The growing light, though still a voice remained,

"Now that you know you're dreaming, you can't stay.
    Wake up and raise your eyelids now." "All right."
"Goodbye." It vanishes, but I can't say
    The others do – I wish they would. The night-
Engendered figures which my guide made play
    Turn small and black like insects on the white
Pages in front of me, a swarming pile
That quickly forms itself to rank and file –

Words on the page: we end where we began.
    Reader, I hope you won't think that's a cop-out,
To give the story with the girl and man,
    Then let the allegory's meaning drop out.
But that's for you to work out if you can.
    Significances don't exactly pop out,
I must admit; but then that's half the fun,
The speculative currant in the bun

Of formula. Abrasive and Ms B.
    And Savage Irony: they could be Twain,
Or Dickens, as your fancy takes you. Me,
    I think they're *Babbitt*, as I could explain
If there were time and space; but as for me,
I'm out of puff – and here's the rhyme again.
I really have to stop. To those who've read
All this, my thanks. And now I'm off to bed.

READER'S GUIDE

(i) W. H. AUDEN

Early Auden

The reader approaching these verses
Should know about sinister nurses,
Be familiar with dreams
And their Freudian themes,
And tell trouser-pockets from purses.

Late Auden

Since the metres deployed in each poem
May vary, make sure that you know 'em
   And, if you are able,
Know Alice from Mabel,
And how xylem differs from phloem.

(ii) WOMEN WRITERS OF THE 1930s
   after Gavin Ewart

Ah! did you see Virginia plain,
   And Laura riding words,
When authors took sides over Spain
   And poets sang like birds?

Did you read Vera's *Testament,*
   And Winifred's *South Riding,*
And Rebecca West on what history meant,
   And all three *Time and Tide*-ing?

When lovely Rosamond Lehmann came
    To Naomi's Boat Race parties,
While Queenie Leavis damned them both
    As snobbish female smarties?

And PEN was run by Storm *mit Drang*,
    And Queenie called it tawdry
That *Dusty Answer* made a bang,
    And Oxford nights were gaudy?

Did you see Stevie Smith in shorts
    Leading her dark chimera,
Or Freya setting starkly forth
    With mule and Arab bearer,

Or Sylvia breathing smoke and wit
    From unexpected angles,
Or Nancy swiping Her Ladyship
    With African ivory bangles?

All gone from us except their books,
    That deathless second-best.
Yes, but the housemaids, typists, cooks,
    Do we forget the rest?

ILLUMINATIONS 1776–1991

The night when Allied planes started to bomb Iraq
I was writing next day's lecture on Edgeworth's *Castle Rackrent*,
until one a.m., far away from Baghdad
lit up by flares, 'like the best Fourth of July ever'
said one American pilot. Yes, those radiant golden
fountains and fiery plumes bursting, cracking, re-forming
in the violent air over falling towers, were a brilliant spectacle.
What fireworks celebrating 'self-evident truths that men
are created equal' could compete? At six a.m. I got up
to finish describing the work of Maria and Richard Edgeworth,
progressive Irish gentry, and their hope for reform.
Richard admired reason and technological progress:
a friend of Joseph Priestley, he invented an early bicycle,
believed in Enlightenment values and human happiness.
So did his daughter Maria, author of Regency novels
notable for their candour, not in our sense of frankness
but the generous impartiality of an enlightened mind,
candor originally being the Latin word for brightness.
Maria's writing was full of morals and elegant prose
like a more progressive Jane Austen (whom in her day she
    outshone)
and pioneered dialect speech, well before Walter Scott...

My lecture was due at eleven. Before it, like all my colleagues
who happened not to be teaching, I went to the Common Room
to watch the war on TV. Our bombs were knocking out
airfields, power and telephones. The US fleet of cruise missiles
(against which I'd once carried banners) were flying through
    Baghdad,
past the BBC reporter's window, he said with excited awe.
Smart bombs were aimed, he told us, with lethal accuracy –
untruly, it turned out later. Candour had become history
which far outshone the lecture I duly gave at eleven

as bombs exploded elsewhere. For what interested my audience
was not Enlightenment values, nor the Rackrents' deserved
    misfortunes,
still less Irish dialect, but the information that Frances,
fourth and final wife of Maria's much-married father,
outlived her stepdaughter, dying one hundred and twenty-four
    years
after Richard Lovell Edgeworth first saw the light of day.

OCCASIONAL POEMS

(i) Prothalamion for Tim and Maggie Cawkwell, 15 January 1972

Some time ago I promised you a sequel
    When last I wrote to you in rhyming stanzas
And here it comes. It can't of course be equal
    To this sublime occasion – Sancho Panzas
    Prefer to stick to beanos and bonanzas,
And this colloquial slangy monologue is
Less near to Arthur's Table than the Cloggies.

For earthy and subversive peasanthood
    (I owe that second adjective to Mary)
Whose main ideas are bed and booze and food,
    Being such vulgarians, should perhaps be wary,
    Not to say shy, reluctant, cautious, chary
When they approach a topic such as this:
– I realise I've not told you what it is.

Well then, to end preliminary disclaimers
    Mainly inspired by C. S. Lewis' writing,
My wish is now to celebrate the famous
    Great, joyous noble – my heart is inditing
    Of a good matter, even to the citing
Of Psalmist scripture – let us not be prim:
The wedding day of MARGARET and TIM.

O happy day! when HETH'RINGTON of BECKENHAM
   Shall be united with OXONIAN CAWKWELL!
What joys shall fall, more fast than I can reckon 'em!
   What bottles of champagne we shall uncork well!
   What hosts of brilliant wedding guests shall talk well!
What sounding anthems shall be raised to HIM
ABOVE, for joy of MARGARET and TIM!

Blest couple! What fair children shall be born
   To grace what Milton calls the genial bed!
As fruitful shall ye be as fields of corn
   When grains shall swell and fill the nodding head,
   More fair than can in verse like this be said!
I know not if it shall be her or him,
But sweet the child of MARGARET and TIM.

I could go on – perhaps you'd like me to –
   And prophesy of infants that shall come,
Sweet babes with hair of gold and eyes of blue,
   Lithe striplings growing up beside their Mum
   And dear Papa – but no, I am struck dumb.
My falt'ring fingers never can begin
To paint the child of MARGARET and TIM.

(ii) To a friend who was out when I called

I meant to do myself the honour
Of calling on you, Ms O'Connor.
What hopes were dashed, what dreams were burnt
When up I went and there you weren't.
If you've been on a holiday,
I hope it was comme tu voudrais;
Ac si tu verba scriberas,
I hope your writing was a gas
And have no doubt but that it was.
I've finished with the dentist's drill
(Thank God) and won't be back until
The rising sun across the bay
Dawns on September's seventh day.
– Distrust all statements made in rhyme.
There is no bay; what's more, the time
Is given wrong, I shall come back
September sixth, so see you then
I hope – although you know the lack
Of rhyme is not a guarantee
Per se of authenticity.
The signifiers blandly play
Between the lines of 'mean' and 'say'
Where, pondering that interface,
The reader views an empty space.

After all that, please remember
We'll meet up some time in September.

(iii) On the Grene family's departure to Dublin,

LIVERPOOL grieves to see you go
And scarcely can contain its woe.
The WIRRAL mourns; unwonted dark
Shadows the groves of SEFTON PARK.
The busts of WILLIAM RATHBONE droop,
The LIVER BIRDS moan in their coop,
The FERRY sinks down to its gunwales
And browner glooms enshroud the TUNNELS.
With the departure of sweet Sophy
BIRKENHEAD's lost its brightest trophy,
Compounded with the loss of Eleanor!
Never since Goering's ordnance fell on her
Has MERSEY known such devastation.

But in the West, what jubilation!
Full of joy and free from care,
Both PHOENIX PARK, MERRION SQUARE
And the great Library of TRINITY
Welcome you back to their vicinity,
And COUNTY WICKLOW'S rural scene
Shall greet you with its brightest green.
The Harp that once in Tara's hall
Sweetened all ears, to greet you all,
Shall sound the best tune known to man.
Goodbye, dear Nicky.
      Love from Jan.

(iv) To a professor of pharmacology, recently knighted

How your laboratory will
Delightedly receive you, Bill!
The instruments shall all unite
To greet Sir William Paton, Knight.
Each compound drug shall rise and stand
To clap a metaphoric hand,
Pipettes shall warble merrily,
Beakers reply in major key,
Retorts respond harmoniously.
And in the test-tube's deep interior
The multitudinous bacteria
Signal to you, through unfamiliar
Spirallings of their sweeping cilia
(It being most appropriate
Since all their names are Latinate,
For bugs to use the language they
Are called by, on this special day):
Gulielme, o doctissime,
Laudamus te fortissime!

So ev'ry note shall join, and be
A scientist's polyphony.

JOHN BETJEMAN BIKING THE GREENWAY, BETWEEN SHOWERS

Sparrows chatter in the ivy
    Shrouding walls and glassless panes
Of the signal-box where lively
    Children in the 'bathing' train,
Eager for the wide and sunny
Seagull-haunted sands of Clonea,
Once would pass with gay elation
Durrow & Stradbally station,
    Roofless now in August rain.

Girls in shorts and boys in yellow
    Hi-vis jackets glide along
Gradients where the train from Mallow
    Once would sing its rhythmic song,
Pistons driving, engine chuffing
Through the ferny moss-grown cutting,
Through the dark now pierced by shining
I-phones held by cyclists riding
    Through the tunnel arched and strong.

By speeding riders overtaken,
    Gorgeous teenagers, I strain
Panting like an over-laden,
    Underpowered, coal truck train
After tanned legs swiftly pumping,
Slim and strong, my senses jumping,
Hypnotised by gold hair streaming
Bare brown thighs and tank tops gleaming
    From Dungarvan in the rain.

On the parapet of Durrow
   Viaduct, red knapweed flowers,
Clover, vetch and seeding yarrow
   Where its seven arches tower.
Wide the amber-flowing river
Tay below where ash-trees shiver,
Green the hayfields and the meadows
Green and cool with summer shadows,
   Cool and green with summer showers.

Up and onward winds the asphalt.
   Legs once muscly, now like lard:
Twelve kilometres twice over
   In the wet, is much too hard.
Stronger limbs than mine may pedal
Undeterred by shower or puddle,
Clad in shorts or Lycra-suited
Where Kilmeaden's steam trains hooted,
   Vapour fading to a puff.

NOTES

p. 31 *The Lecturer's Dream* was inspired by the experience of teaching an undergraduate course on 'The Novel' at the University of Liverpool in the 1970s, covering the canon of fiction, as then defined, from Defoe to Henry James plus selected French and Russian novelists. In our weekly lectures and tutorials we taught the work of nearly every writer mentioned here. The names in the card game are derived from phrases often used in student essays.

p. 34 *pleonast*: one who commits a superfluity of words.

p. 41 *The Cloggies:* 1970s strip cartoon by Bill Tidy in *Private Eye*. Mary: Mary Jacobus, then Research Fellow at Lady Margaret Hall, Oxford, who had taught Shakespeare to Maggie and myself. C.S. Lewis' writing: *The Allegory of Love*.

p. 46 *the 'bathing' train:* During the 1940s and 50s, the Waterford to Dungarvan railway ran cheap summer day excursions, known as 'bathing trains', to the seaside village Clonea.